SHAKE UP
SCIENCE 2

Pearson Education Limited
Edinburgh Gate
Harlow
Essex CM20 2JE
England
and Associated Companies throughout the world.

www.pearsonelt.com

© Pearson Education Limited 2016

First published 2016
ISBN: 978-1-2921-4472-6
Set in Futura LT Pro, Feltpen Com, Bauhaus Std, ITC Benguiat Gothic Std, ITC Zapf Dingbats Std
Printed in China (CTPSC/02)

Acknowledgments
Picture Credits
The publisher would like to thank the following for their kind permission to reproduce their photographs:

(Key: b-bottom; c-centre; l-left; r-right; t-top)

123RF.com: 6c, 6cr, 13r, 16 (eggs), 16tl, 16tc, 16cl, 27tr, 27cr, 30tl, 41c (right), 41bl, 43c, 43br, 45l, 52tc, 52tr, 52cl, 76bl, 88 (clock), 93 (jar), 93c, 100tl, 100tc (left), 100c (right), 101b, Serge Bertasius 30c, greggr 76tl, Alessio Orrù 16 (cheese), pzaxe 64tl; **Alamy Images:** Foodcollection 10tr; **Fotolia.com:** ambrozinio 48br, andriano_cz 94bc (left), BillionPhotos.com 52 (ring), bit24 42cr, Charles Butzin 52 (spear), Cheryl Davis 96cr, flairimages 47tr, freshidea 49bc (left), Warren Goldswain 48bc (left), Gorilla 48bc (right), isoga 60bl, larcobasso 40tr, Pavel Losevsky 48tr, Niki Love 49bl, mettus 48bl, Elena Milevska 49bc (right), 51bc (left), MNStudio 48cr, 51br, mylisa 93 (bowl), ognianmed 93cl, ptasha 94br, Kimberly Reinick 47b, Mauro Rodrigues 53cr, Evgeny Skidanov 96r, TuTheLens 49br, Beth Van Trees 46t, Vitalinka 43bc 45c; **Getty Images:** Mark Stay 15br; **Imagemore Co., Ltd:** 4tl; **Imagestate Media:** John Foxx Collection 44b; **Pearson Education Ltd:** Lisa Payne Photography 106l; **SF Glenview Photo Studio:** 14, 26, 38, 62, 74, 86, 98, 110; **Shutterstock.com:** 2xSamara.com 43cr, 105bl, 7Horses 27bc, abimages 16c (right), Johnny Adolphson 103br, Africa Studio 81tr, Ermolaev Alexander 34t, Ozerov Alexander 73 (background), Vasilyev Alexandr 65t, altanaka 51tr, Volnukhin Anatoly 33tr, Andrey_Kuzmin 12bl, apdesign 100c (left), Artmim 6l, Aspen Photo 95bl,

aztekphoto 9c, B747 67t, 75t, Lester Balajadia 70b, Andrey N Bannov 22bc, 27br, Andrey Bayda 89t, Mircea Bezergheanu 93cr, bikeriderlondon 57r, 63t, Bildagentur Zoonar GmbH 72t, Jon Bilous 54 (background), Barry Blackburn 70cr, BlueOrange Studio 61l, 61r, BMJ 88c, Anna Bogush 33tl, Natalia Bratslavsky 9t, Simon Bratt 100cr, Darryl Brooks 68bc, 75c, burnel1 64cr, Danette Carnahan 22r, cath5 73cr, Jacek Chabraszewski 96l, chbaum 58b, Hung Chung Chih 41c (left), choikh 29cr, Robert Cicchetti 67b, cyo bo 28cr, D7INAMI7S 81l, Vladyslav Danilin 52bc, James DeBoer 32r, design56 64br, Digital Media Pro 105tc, Eaglesky 17t, Elena Elisseeva 88 (plane), evan66 60cr, fad82 6cl, Konstantin Faraktinov 50l, 88tr, Tausif Farooqi 17br, feathercollector 31r, Patrick Foto 64bl, Fotofermer 42r, Fremme 52br, g215 18, Gelpi JM 96cl, Gemenacom 44t, Pashin Georgiy 28tr, Eric Gevaert 28bc, Monika Gniot 100tc (right), goldnetz 93 (napkin), Warren Goldswain 107, Johanna Goodyear 76tr, Nicole Gordine 84t, gorillaimages 41cr, Mr. Green 16 (wool), Arto Hakola 22l, Josef Hanus 50r, Steve Heap 59, Jiri Hera 17cl, 40tl, hin255 27bl, Jiang Hongyan 88 (iron), Horiyan 88tl, Alex Hubenov 37, Hurst Photo 88 (fan), hxdbzxy 41cl, Francesco R. Iacomino 56cr, Maxim Ibragimov 91bc, Miks Mihails Ignats 55r, ilike 4c, imagedb.com 91bl, Inessa_N 5br, Irena13 85r, Eric Isselee 28tl, Ivancovlad 4bl, Marcel Jancovic 104b, JanHetman 16cr, Nick Jay 88 (flowers), Rosa Jay 33b, 39c, Matt Jeppson 32c, Tomo Jesenicnik 16bc, Jessmine 15cr, Jiripravda 5bl, JL Jahn 22 (background), Joel_420 70cl, 75cr, Magnum Johansson 77, Dmitry Kalinovsky 28br, 56tr, 94tl, Agnes Kantaruk 93tr, kavram 66b, Sergey Kelin 71cr, Trevor Kelly 71br, Levent Konuk 29 (clownfish), Lev Kropotov 88cl, kurhan 7, kzww 4b, Doug Lemke 29tr, Daniel Leppens 101c, 103bl, LiAndStudio 35r, Dmitriev Lidiya 64tr, Varit Limwibul 54l, Lena Lir 100tr, Lizard 58l, Mike Loiselle 19t, lola1960 8b, Anatoliy Lukich 29 (cat), Andrew Lundquist 104c, Madlen 54r, Paul Maguire 94bc (right), Markus Mainka 16bl, majeczka 8t, Gabriele Maltinti 55b, mangostock 49tr, 51bc (right), MarcelClemens 76br, Marques 42l, MartinMaritz 23b, V. J. Matthew 35l, Joe McDonald 11l, Oleg Mikhaylov 105tr, Jan Miko 31l, William Milner 88 (chair), Alex Mit 68br, Monkey Business Images 43bl, 69b, monticello 76cr, Al Mueller 31c, Andrii Muzyka 55c, n_eri 92tc, Namning 76cl, Nando 5bc, neelsky 56br, Oleg Nekhaev 29 (goldfish), NicVW 56bl, nikitsin. smugmug.com 91tr, nikkytok 17c, 103tr, Sergey Novikov 108, 109b, pakowacz 13l, panbazil 34b, Anita Patterson Peppers 92br, Paul Matthew Photography 9 (background), Pavel L Photo and Video 49cr, 68t, Andrey Pavlov 32l, Sean Pavone 102b, pchais 53l, PHB.cz (Richard Semik) 103tl, Loo Joo Pheng 29 (panther), 39t, phofotos 92cr, photo.ua 94tr, photolinc 65br, pio3 97l, pjcross 60cl, 93bl, plavevski 28bl, Olga Popova 64c (left), Malte Pott 65cr, Pressmaster 102t, Lee Prince 57l, Quaoar 52cr, racorn 6tr, 15tr, Sergej Razvodovskij 89b, Tom Reichner 12 (background), 20b, 21 (background), 29bl, Rohappy 104t, Martina Roth 53cl, sakkmesterke 40b, samarttiw 60 (background), 63b, Tim Scott 42cl, scyther5 90, Ruslan Semichev 84c, serg_dibrova 99, Ilin Sergey (stopwatch), Zvyagintsev Sergey 4br, sfam_photo 94bl, Andrei Shumskiy 12br, Marcio Jose Bastos Silva 101t, Sinelyov 28cl, sl_photo 64c (right), smereka 9b, Smit 71t, 75b, Ljupco Smokovski 51bl, Kent Sorensen 30b, Lori Sparkia 84l, srekap 30tr, Sergio Stakhnyk 68bl, 75cl, Florin Stana 106r, STILLFX 12cl, Alexey Stiop 16c (left), stockcreations 88b, Minerva Studio 66t, studioVin 88cr, Sujono sujono 69t, sunsinger

20t, Syda Productions 81br, Taiga 72b, Tania A 52tl, tarasov 52bl, Tatiana53 23t, 33cr, Charles Taylor 91br, Winai Tepsuttinun 76c, Kenny Tong 16tr, TonLammerts 85l, Max Topchii 55t, topseller 46b, Triff 88tc, TrotzOlga 64cl, Suzanne Tucker 47tr, Vinicius Tupinamba 60br, Rudy Umans 24, UMB-O 92tl, Martin Valigursky 105tl, Eva Vargyasi 95r, Dmytro Vietrov 111, Vikulin 97r, Vitalinka 45r, Vaclav Volrab 36, 39b, VR Photos 17c, VVO 53r, Craig Wactor 10bl, Tom Wang 100b, wavebreakmedia 5t, 19b, 40tc, WDG Photo 109t, withGod 29br, Jolanta Wojcicka 25, A v.d. Wolde 6r, John Wollwerth 43t, Worldpics 16br, Yaping 12cr, yevgeniy11 15cl, Feng Yu 4tr, 11r, 12bc, Peter Zijlstra 21, zukerka 100cl

All other images © Pearson Education

Every effort has been made to trace the copyright holders and we apologize in advance for any unintentional omissions. We would be pleased to insert the appropriate acknowledgment in any subsequent edition of this publication.

Science Consultant
Mark Sander

Illustrated by
Marcela Gómez Ruenes **18**c, **67**c, **75**t, Andrés Morales **45**tr, **46**tr, **47**cr, **48**cr, **49**cr, **94**b

Cover images: Front: Getty Images: monkeybusinessimages r; Shutterstock.com: S. Kuelcue l; Back: Shutterstock.com: Ozerov Alexander c, hin255 l, Sergey Novikov r

Contents

The Design Process

 **How do you solve problems?**

I will learn

- how technology helps people solve problems.
- what materials different objects are made of.
- to explain the design process.

1 Look and circle the tools they are using.

stapler

nails

hammer

scissors

screwdriver

2 Think of something you want to make. Name the tools you will need.

 Think!

What are the father and son in this picture making?

Lesson 1 · What is technology?

1 **Read, look, and mark (✔) the tool the boy is using.**

Key Words

- technology
- science
- scientist
- discovery

Technology

Technology is using **science** to help solve problems. Computers are a kind of technology. **Scientists** use technology to make **discoveries**. Sometimes scientists discover new technologies.

Technology helps scientists to do their work.

☐ computer   ☐ tablet   ☐ cell phone

2 **Do we use all these inventions now? Say as a class.**

1870
The first all metal bicycle.

1876
The first telephone call.

1946
The first computer.

③ Read and underline a problem that technology solves.

Solve Problems

Technology helps people solve problems. One problem is that people need to communicate with each other. They might not be in the same place. They can use a telephone. A telephone is technology.

The boy uses a pencil to communicate. A pencil is technology.

④ Look and circle other examples of technology.

⑤ Look at the timeline on page 5. Number the inventions 1, 2, or 3 in the order they were invented.

[ ] telephone   [ ] bicycle

[ ] computer

Think!

what would you like to invent?

6 Read. What are three kinds of technology a car can have? Say with a partner.

Staying Safe

Technology helps people stay safe. People use cars to get from place to place. Seat belts and airbags help make cars safe. Safety seats help children keep safe in a car.

Technology helps people stay safe in cars.

7 Draw another kind of technology that helps people solve problems.

Go Green

Helping Earth
Think of a technology that helps keep the air or water clean. Tell how it helps.

Lesson 2 · What are objects made of?

1 Read. Look and point to three objects in the park that people made.

Different Materials

People use **materials** to make objects. Some materials are natural. **Natural** means not made by people. Materials that come directly from Earth are natural. **Wood** and **cotton** are natural. **Rocks** and minerals are natural, too. Sometimes people use natural materials to make new materials. **Plastic** is a material people make.

2 Look at the photo. Circle one material that is natural and cross out (✗) one material that is made by people.

3 Read. Look and color the frame around the materials you might use to build a house.

Natural Materials

Natural materials are different from each other. People use them in different ways. Wood and rocks are hard. People use them to make buildings. Cotton is soft. People use cotton to make clothes.

4 Write one kind of material you might use to make a pillow.

_____

_____

5 What material is soft? What materials are hard? Say with a partner.

6 **Read and write two things people can make out of plastic.**

Man-Made Materials

People make new materials, and they use them in different ways. Plastic is a new material. Some plastic is hard, and some plastic is soft. People use more than one material to make some objects. They can use plastic and wood to make a chair.

A plastic cup can hold food or a drink.

Packing foam is a soft type of plastic.

Flash Lab

Materials

Find two objects. Tell what materials people used to make them. Tell if the materials are natural or people made them.

Lesson 3 · What is the design process?

1 **Read. Circle the problem and underline the goal.**

A Problem and a Goal

Wood ducks are animals that need shelter. First, you set a goal, to design a house for wood ducks. A **goal** is something you want to do. Your house for wood ducks will be a solution. A **solution** solves a **problem**.

Wood ducks do not make their own shelters. They use shelters that people or other animals make.

2 **Draw a house for a wood duck.**

Plan and Draw

Next, you make a **plan** to build your house for wood ducks. You write about how to make your house for wood ducks. You draw what your house for wood ducks will look like.

3 **Read. Look and circle three materials you need to make a house for wood ducks.**

Choose Materials

Next, you decide what materials to use to make your house for wood ducks. You might choose wood for the walls. You might choose nails to hold the walls together. You need something on the inside so the wood ducks can climb out. You might choose a piece of screen.

tape

wood

screen

nails

microphone

4 **Read. How do you know your house for wood ducks works well? Say with a partner.**

Test

Next, you make your house for wood ducks. You check the house every day. You see if wood ducks live there.

5 **Read, look, and label the details of the house for wood ducks.**

Record and Share

You decide how your solution works. You plan again to make your solution better. You write and draw to tell about your solution. You use **labels** to show parts of your solution.

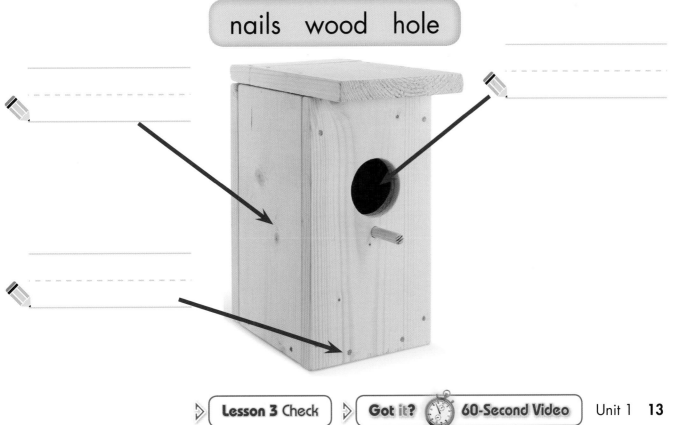

nails   wood   hole

gram cubes

foil

plastic tub of water

Let's Investigate!

How can you build a boat?

1. Design a boat that will float. Draw your design.

2. Build your boat.

3. Add gram cubes to your boat until it sinks. Record.

4. Redesign your boat to hold more cubes. Predict how many gram cubes it will hold before it sinks. Record.

Lesson 1

What is technology?

1 Circle the word that best completes the sentence.

Technology helps solve _____.

goals   solutions   problems   science

Lesson 2

What are objects made of?

2 Circle the object with no natural materials.

Lesson 3

What is the design process?

3 How can you test an ant farm? Underline the answer.

a. put food inside

c. draw the ant farm

b. tell about the ant farm

d. see if ants live there

Unit 2

Living Things and Their Environments

THE BIG ? **What do plants and animals need?**

I will learn

- what living things need.
- how plants and animals can live in land and water environments.

1 **Circle where cows live.**

forest

pasture

desert

2 **Cross out (x) what a cow does not need.**

3 **Look and circle the products we get from cows. Think of two more.**

Think!

Why do cows need the sun?

Lesson 1 · What do living things need?

1 **Look and draw one missing thing that the plant needs to grow. Read.**

Key Words

- need
- air
- water
- light
- nutrients
- soil
- shelter

Needs

All living things have needs. A **need** is something a living thing must have to live. Plants and animals are living things. They have needs. People have needs, too.

Poppy plants have needs.

Needs of Plants

Plants need **air** and **water**. They need **light** to make food. They need space to live and grow.

2 **Why do the poppy plants look healthy? Talk about it as a class.**

Flash Lab

Play a Plant

Sit on the floor.
Raise both hands.
You are a plant.
You get no water.
Slowly show what happens.

3 **Read. Look and point to where the strawberry plants get nutrients.**

Nutrients

Plants need nutrients. **Nutrients** are materials that living things need. Plants can get nutrients from the **soil**.

4 **Why do strawberry plants need nutrients? Say with a partner.**

5 **Look and complete the chart.**

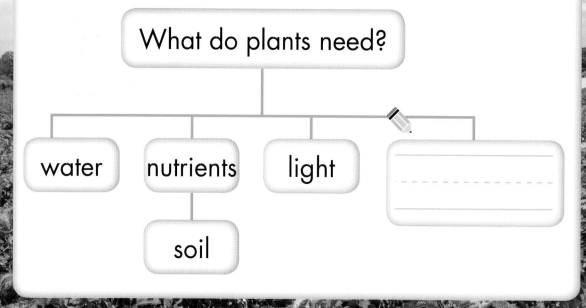

What do plants need?

- water
- nutrients
  - soil
- light
- _____

6 **Read. What do animals and people need? Say with a partner.**

Beavers build their own shelter.

Needs of Animals

Animals need air, water, and food.
They get nutrients from food.
Animals need space to live.
Some animals need shelter.
Shelter is a safe place.

Needs of People

People need air, water, and food.
They get nutrients from food.
People need space to live. They need shelter. Shelter keeps them warm and dry.

7 **Match what plants and animals need.**

plants   animals

air   light   soil

food   shelter   water

Lesson 2 · How do plants and animals live in land environments?

1 **Read. Look at the picture and say two things you think are in the horses' environment.**

Key Words

- environment
- forest
- prairie
- desert

Environments

An **environment** is all the living and nonliving things in one place. It has food, water, and air. Land is one kind of environment. Land has rocks and soil. Many plants and animals live on land.

2 **Read. With a partner, describe the forest.**

Forest Environments

A **forest** is a land environment. It is land that has many trees and other plants. Black bears live in some forests. They have sharp claws. Bears use their claws to dig for food. Sharp claws help bears climb trees.

Think!

why did the bear climb the tree?

③ Read. Cross out (✗) one thing you will not find in the prairies.

Prairie Environment

A **prairie** is a land environment. It is flat land that is covered with grasses. Prairie dogs live in some prairies. They have sharp teeth. Sharp teeth help them chew the prairie grass. Prairie dogs have sharp claws, too. They help them dig holes in the ground. They use holes for shelter.

grass

mountains

prairie dogs

plants

④ Circle the part of the prairie dog that helps it dig holes.

5 **Read. With a partner, say words that describe deserts.**

Desert Environment

A **desert** is a land environment. It is land that is very dry. It gets very little rain or snow. Most deserts are very hot; others are very cold. Plants grow in deserts. Plants in deserts hold water. Many animals get the water they need from the plants they eat.

6 **Read. Circle the parts of the rabbit, the plant, and the lizard that help keep them cool.**

Heat leaves the rabbit's body through its big ears.

This desert is hot during the day. Light-colored skin helps this lizard stay cool.

Waxy leaves help this plant hold water.

Lesson 2 Check   Got it?   60-Second Video

Lesson 3 · How do plants and animals live in water environments?

1 **Read. With a partner, talk about how some plants float on water.**

Key Words
- wetland • swamp
- marsh • ocean

Water Environments

Some animals live in water environments. They get what they need there. Some plants live in water environments, too. Flat leaves help the plants float. Long stems with roots down to the soil soak up the nutrients. Some plants live underwater.

2 **Read. Circle two parts of the heron that help it live in the marsh.**

Marsh Environments

A **wetland** is an environment that is covered with water. **Marshes** are wetlands, and they have grasses. Many different kinds of animals live in marshes. Blue herons live in marshes. They have long, sharp beaks, and they catch fish with them. Herons have long, thin legs, too.

3 **Read. Why do alligators in a swamp need to be good swimmers? Say with a partner.**

Swamp Environment

Swamps are wetlands. A **swamp** has soft, wet land and many trees. Alligators live in some swamps. They are good swimmers. They use their long, strong tails to help them swim.

4 **Make a list of other animals you can find in a marsh or a swamp.**

5 Read. Underline the sentence that tells how gills help fish live in the ocean.

Ocean Environment

An **ocean** is a large body of salty water. Some parts of the ocean are deep. Fish live in the ocean. They have gills. Gills let fish take in oxygen from the water. Fish have fins, which help them swim.

Plants need sunlight to make food. Ocean plants live where there is light. The deep ocean is dark. Plants do not live there.

6 Draw an **x** on the parts of the fish that help it swim.

7 Why don't plants live in the deep ocean? Say as a class.

2 cups
with grass

water

Let's Investigate!

Why do plants need light?

1. Water both plants. Draw both plants in a chart to record what you observe.

2. Put one cup in sunlight. Put one cup in a dark place.

3. Check the plants every day. Draw both plants after 1 week.

Lesson 1

What do living things need?

1 Read and match.

a) They get nutrients from food.

b) They use light to make food.

Lesson 2

How do plants and animals live in land environments?

2 Circle what best completes the sentence.

_____ help bears live in the forest.

Gills   Sharp claws   Big ears   Light-colored skin

Lesson 3

How do plants and animals live in water environments?

3 Cross out (✗) the animal that does not live in a wetland environment.

Unit 3

Plants and Animals

How are living things alike and different?

I will learn

- ways to group living things.
- how living things are like their parents.
- how living things are alike and different.

1 Match the babies with their parents. Which animal is different from its parent? Say as a class.

puppy

cat

kitten

panda bear

newborn panda

dog

Think!

How is a young orangutan like its mother?

Lesson 1 · What are some groups of living things?

Key Words

- seed
- cone
- backbone
- mammal
- reptile
- amphibian
- insect

1 **Read. Compare and contrast the cardinal and the betta fish. Circle *Yes* or *No*.**

Groups of Living Things

Plants and animals are living things. You can group them in different ways. For example, you can group them by size, color, or shape. Scientists group living things, too.

cardinal

a) Are they both living things?   **Yes / No**

b) Do they have the same shape? **Yes / No**

c) Do they both swim?   **Yes / No**

d) Are they both red?   **Yes / No**

betta fish

2 **With a partner, say different ways you can group the animals in the pictures.**

    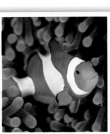 

3 **Read. What are two ways to classify plants? Say with a partner.**

Plants with Flowers

There are two main plant groups. One group of plants grows flowers. The other group does not grow flowers. Plants with flowers make **seeds**. Seeds grow in the flowers. Plants with flowers grow in many places.

Plants without Flowers

Some plants do not have flowers. Some plants have **cones**. Seeds grow inside the cones. Some plants do not have flowers or cones. These plants do not make any seeds. They often grow in wet places.

4 **Match the texts with the pictures.**

Flowers grow on some trees.

Moss does not make seeds.

Pine trees have cones.

5 **Read and circle one group of animals that has backbones.**

Animal Groups

One group of animals has backbones. A **backbone** is the set of bones along the middle of the back. **Mammals** are animals with backbones. Most mammals have fur or hair.

Birds have backbones. Birds are covered with feathers and have wings. Fish have backbones. Fish live in water and have scales.

moose

oriole

rockfish

6 **Match the animals with their group.**

Animal	Group
canary	mammal
cow	
goldfish	fish
parrot	
orangutan	bird

Think!

Do a moose, an oriole, and a rockfish have backbones? Why?

7 **Read. What is an animal group that does not have backbones? Say with a partner.**

More Animal Groups

Reptiles have backbones. Most reptiles have dry skin and scales.

Amphibians have backbones. They have smooth, wet skin.

Another group of animals does not have backbones. This is the largest group of animals. **Insects** are part of this group. All insects have six legs.

8 **Which group does each animal belong to? Talk about it as a class.**

ant

salamander

turtle

Lesson 2 · How are living things like their parents?

Key Words
- parent
- young
- alike
- shape
- different

1 **Read. Look and match the young plant with its parent.**

Plants and Their Parents

A **parent** is a living thing that has **young**. Plants and their parents are **alike**. They can have the same leaf **shape**. Plants and their parents are **different**, too. They can have different colored flowers.

2 **Read. With a partner, tell how the dog and its parent are alike.**

How Animals and Their Parents Are Alike

Young animals are like their parents. Many animals look like their parents. They have the same shape as their parents. Animals and their parents can have the same number of legs.

3 **Read. How are the cat and its kitten different? Say with a partner.**

How Animals and Their Parents Are Different

Young animals and their parents are different, too. They can be different colors. Young animals are smaller than their parents.

At-Home Lab

Parents and Young

Find a picture of an animal and its young. Glue it to a sheet of paper. Write how your animals are alike and different.

4 **Look at the chickens. Mark (✔) the sentences that tell how the chicks are different from their parent.**

They are small. ☐

They have two legs. ☐

They are yellow. ☐

Lesson 3 · How are groups of living things different?

Key Words
- petunia
- fuzzy
- herd

① Read. Circle the words that describe petunia leaves.

Kinds of Plants

Plants live all around the world. Plants of one kind are alike. **Petunias** are a kind of plant. They all have **fuzzy**, green leaves. Plants of one kind are different, too.

② Look at the pictures. Write how the petunias are alike and different.

> pink   leaves

a) How are the petunias alike?

They both have green _____.

b) How are the petunias different?

One petunia has _____ flowers.

③ Read. Underline ways that giraffes are alike.

Kinds of Animals

Animals of one kind are alike. Giraffes are a kind of animal. The picture shows a herd of giraffes. A **herd** is a group of animals of one kind that stays together. Giraffes have four legs and two eyes. They have spots, too.

④ Draw another giraffe in the herd. Tell how it is the same as the others.

5 **Read. Fill in the words *long*, *spots*, and *short*.**

Different Animals of One Kind

Animals of one kind are different, too. Some giraffes have darker spots than others. Some giraffes have longer necks than others. Giraffes with longer necks can reach leaves on tall trees. Short giraffes cannot reach as high.

Across

1. _____ giraffes cannot reach as high.

Down

2. _____ necks help giraffes reach leaves.

3. The _____ on some giraffes are darker.

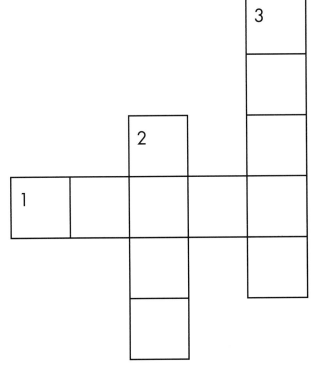

Flash Lab

Alike and Different

Think of two of the same kind of plant or animal. Tell how they are alike. Tell how they are different.

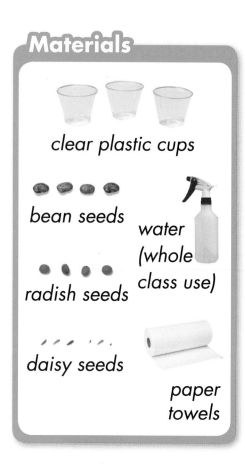

clear plastic cups

bean seeds

water
(whole
class use)

radish seeds

daisy seeds

paper
towels

Let's Investigate!

How do different seeds grow?

1. Fold a paper towel.
Put it inside a cup.

2. Wet the paper towel with water.

3. Put the bean seeds in the cup.

4. Repeat the steps with radish seeds.
Repeat the steps with daisy seeds.

5. Observe the seeds for 10 days.
Draw what you see.
Use the Seed Growth Chart.

REVIEW THE BIG ? How are living things alike and different?

Lesson 1

What are some groups of living things?

1 Circle the group of animals that has fur or hair.

a. reptiles   c. mammals

b. birds   d. insects

Lesson 2

How are living things like their parents?

2 Underline the ways the puppy and its parent are alike.

a. They are the same color.

b. They have the same shape.

c. They are the same size.

d. They have the same number of legs.

Lesson 3

How are groups of living things different?

3 Mark (✔) the ways giraffes in the same herd can be different.

☐ Some giraffes have shorter necks.

☐ Some giraffes have no tails.

☐ Some giraffes have darker spots.

Unit 4

Body and Health

 **What do I need to be healthy?**

1 **Look and label the pictures.**

helmet   vegetables   soap

2 **Are these things good for you or bad for you? Discuss as a class.**

3 **Draw another thing that is good for you.**

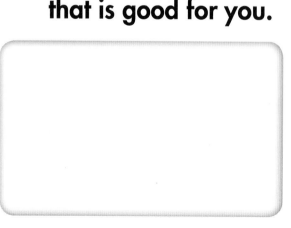

Think!

Why does your body need water?

Lesson 1 · What can I do to stay healthy?

Key Words
- healthy
- exercise
- habit
- cavity
- eating well
- check up

1 **Read and match the pictures to the healthy habits.**

Healthy Habits

Your body is an amazing thing. It is important to take care of your body. Good habits help keep your body **healthy**. A **habit** is something that you do again and again. Some good habits are eating good food, exercising, sleeping, keeping your body clean, and going to the doctor.

exercising   eating good food   keeping clean   sleeping

2 **Mark (✔) two unhealthy things this girl is doing.**

☐ exercising   ☐ eating potato chips

☐ drinking soda   ☐ sleeping

3 **Read and circle the two healthy foods. Cross out (✗) the two unhealthy foods.**

Eating Well

You eat food to get energy and nutrients. Your body uses the nutrients to grow and stay healthy.

Eating well means eating different types of food. You can eat meat and fish, beans, vegetables, fruit, and grains like rice and wheat. Milk keeps your bones and teeth strong.

You can have candy as a special treat once in a while. Candy has a lot of sugar. Too much sugar can be bad for you.

4 **Draw your lunch. Is it healthy? Compare with a partner.**

5 Read the text and circle *T* (true) or *F* (false).

Exercising

You get **exercise** every time you play soccer, run around the playground, or walk to school. Exercise is important because it keeps your heart, bones, and muscles healthy.

What happens when you exercise? Your heart beats faster. You breathe faster, too!

Swimming is good exercise.

Climbing makes your muscles stronger.

Hopping keeps your bones strong.

1. Watching TV is a type of exercise.   T / F

2. Exercise is good for your bones and muscles.   T / F

3. Exercise is bad for your heart.   T / F

4. Your heart beats faster when you exercise.   T / F

6 Circle some ways you exercise. What is another way you exercise? Say with a partner.

walking

running

swimming

7 **Read and circle the child who is getting sleep at night.**

Getting Sleep

It is important for children who are six to 12 years old to sleep for ten to 11 hours each night.

Your body grows when you sleep. Sleep helps your brain understand what you learn during the day. If you don't get enough sleep, you might be in a bad mood and not pay attention in class the next day.

8 **Imagine that you are very tired and need to sleep. Draw yourself.**

9 **Read and circle the pictures that show healthy habits.**

Keeping Clean

It's good to keep your body clean. It is important to take baths or showers regularly. Always take a bath or shower after getting dirty or exercising. Wash your hands with soap after you go to the bathroom and before you eat. Brushing your teeth keeps them clean, too. It helps you not get a **cavity**, or a hole, in your teeth!

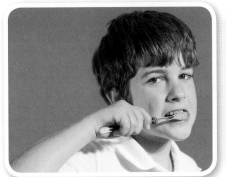  

10 **What do doctors do to help you? Say with a partner.**

Going to the Doctor

Going to the doctor regularly can help you stay healthy. The doctor can give you a check up. A **check up** makes sure you are healthy. The doctor can check how tall you are and how much you weigh. The doctor can listen to your heart. The doctor can also give you vaccinations so you don't get sick.

Lesson 2 · How can I stay healthy and safe?

Key Words

- germs
- sick
- sneeze
- skin
- heal
- cut
- bandage
- helmet
- life jacket

1 **Read. Number the steps (1–4) to show how you can get sick.**

Wash Your Hands

Healthy habits help keep your body strong. There are other things you can do to keep yourself healthy.

Germs live everywhere. They can get inside your body and make you **sick**. Washing your hands is the best way to not get sick.

A sick person who **sneezes** spreads germs in the air. Germs get on things that you touch. You get the germs on your hands. When you touch your mouth, nose, or eyes, you can get sick, too!

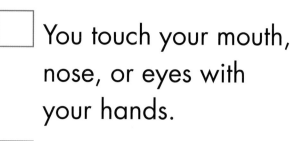

☐ Germs land on something you touch.

☐ You touch your mouth, nose, or eyes with your hands.

☐ You get germs on your hands.

☐ A sick person sneezes.

② Read the text and circle *T* (true) or *F* (false).

Clean Cuts

Your **skin** is very good at healing itself. To **heal** means to become healthy again. You can help your skin heal faster when you get a **cut**. Wash it with soap and water to kill any germs. You can cover the cut with a **bandage**. That will help it stay clean. Your skin will heal faster. If you get a really bad cut, go to the doctor.

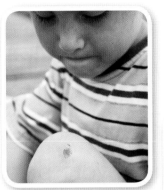

1. Your skin cannot heal itself. **T / F**

2. It is good to wash a cut with soap and water. **T / F**

3. Soap and water do not kill germs. **T / F**

4. Using a bandage on a cut helps it stay clean. **T / F**

③ With a partner, act out getting a cut and how to treat it.

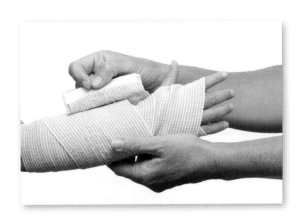

4 **Read and circle what the girls are wearing to stay safe.**

Stay Safe When You Play

There are some easy ways to stay safe when you play. Wear a **helmet** when you ride your bike. It will protect your head if you fall. Stay safe from cars. Don't play or ride your bike in the street. Look both ways when you cross the street. Swimming is good exercise. But it's important to be careful around water. Make sure an adult watches you when you swim. Wear a life jacket when you ride in a boat. A **life jacket** will help you to float if you fall into the water.

5 **Circle the children who are being safe. Cross out (✗) the children who are not being safe.**

6 **Read. With a partner, name two things that protect you from the sun.**

Protect Your Skin and Eyes from the Sun

If you get sunburn, your skin turns red and feels hot. It hurts a lot. Sunscreen is a lotion that will keep your skin safe from the sun.

Put on sunscreen before you go outside. Put on more sunscreen after you go swimming. Wear sunscreen on all the parts of your body that are not covered by clothes.

The sun can also hurt your eyes. Wear sunglasses when it is sunny.

7 **Circle the things you take to the beach that keep you safe.**

Materials

black construction paper

sunscreen lotion

Let's Investigate!

How does sunscreen protect my skin?

1. Fold the black construction paper in half.

2. Put a small amount of sunscreen on the right half of the paper. Rub it around in a circle until it disappears.

3. Lay the paper in the sun.

4. Move the paper so that it stays in the sun all day long.

5. Record your observations at the end of the day.

	Sunscreen	Observations
Left side of paper	no	
Right side of paper	yes	

REVIEW THE BIG ?
What do I need to be healthy?

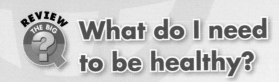

Lesson 1

What should I do to stay healthy?

1 Circle the correct answers.
What are some healthy habits?

a) watching television   b) staying clean

c) drinking soda pop   d) eating well

2 Match the first half of each sentence to the second half.

a) Sleep is important because   your heart healthy.

b) Brushing your teeth helps   it helps your brain
                                                          remember things.

c) Eating well means   you not get
                                                          cavities.

d) Exercise keeps   eating different
                                                          types of food.

Lesson 2

How can I stay healthy and safe?

3 Circle the things that can keep you safe.

Earth and Sky

 What can you say about Earth and sky?

1 Match to show what can be found on Earth or in the sky.

sky   Earth

2 Look at the picture of the rock. Circle the objects made of rock.

Think!

what does the rock look like?

Lesson 1 · What is on Earth?

1 **Read. Color the land green and the water blue.**

Key Words
- plain
- hill
- mountain
- island
- river
- lake

Land, Water, and Air

Earth is made of many things. It has land and water. The surface of Earth has more water than land. Earth has air all around it.

2 **Read. Look and match the pictures to the words.**

Kinds of Land

Earth has many different kinds of land. **Plains** are large, flat areas of land. **Hills** are where the land gets higher. **Mountains** are the highest kind of land. An **island** is land with water all around it.

island   mountain   plain   hill

3 Read. With a partner, say two things that are found on Earth.

Rocks and Soil

Earth's land has rocks and soil. Rocks are hard and can be many colors. Soil is the top layer of Earth. Soil can be soft.

rocks

soil

4 Write one way soil and rocks are different.

soil   rocks

They are both on Earth's land.

At-Home Lab

Kinds of Landforms

Draw one kind of land near where you live. Draw another kind of land. Write how they are the same. Write how they are different.

5 **Read. Look at the pictures. Circle the correct word.**

river / lake

Water on Earth

Earth has many places with water. A **river** is water that flows across land. **Lakes** have land all around them. The ocean is a large area of salt water. It covers most of Earth.

river / lake

ocean / lake

6 **Draw two things that live in the ocean.**

7 **Look at the picture. Circle one living thing on land and one living thing on or in water.**

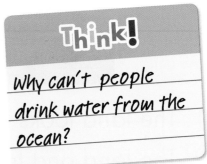

Think!

why can't people drink water from the ocean?

Lesson 2 · What changes land?

1 **Read. Mark (✔) the picture that shows what causes a slow change on Earth.**

Changes on Earth

Earth is always changing. Some changes happen fast. A bulldozer digs a hole in the ground. This is a fast change. Other changes are very slow. A river flows across land. This changes land slowly.

This bulldozer moves rocks and soil.

The Colorado River makes the Grand Canyon deeper and wider.

2 **Look at the photo of the volcano that erupted. Underline the sentence that tells how the land changed.**

1. The land looks dry, and the trees have disappeared.
2. The land and trees look green.

3 **Read. With a partner, talk about what an earthquake can cause.**

Earthquakes and Volcanoes

Earthquakes happen fast. They can cause land to crack. Volcanoes cause fast changes, too. They can explode. Rock and ash from a volcano can cover land.

earthquake

volcano

4 **Complete the sentence that tells how earthquakes and volcanoes are alike. Use a word from the text.**

Earthquakes and volcanoes cause _____ on Earth.

5 **Read. Circle what causes weathering and underline what causes erosion.**

Weathering and Erosion

Weathering and erosion change land slowly. **Weathering** is when water or ice breaks down rocks.

Erosion is when wind or water moves rocks and soil. Weathering and erosion can take a long time!

weathering

erosion

6 **What causes slow land changes? What causes fast land changes? Talk about it as a class.**

Lesson 3 · What is the sun?

1 **Read. Why does the sun look small? Talk about it as a class.**

Key Words

- star
- gas
- warm
- heat
- harm
- sunglasses

The Nearest Star

A **star** is a big ball of hot **gas**. The sun is a star. It is the star that is nearest to Earth. The sun is bigger than Earth. The sun looks small because it is far away.

2 **Circle a warm place to sit in the photo. With a partner, talk about why it is warmer to sit on the bench than to sit under the tree.**

3 **Read. Circle one reason that living things need the sun.**

Why We Need the Sun

The sun helps us. It **warms** the land, the water, and the air. Living things need **heat** from the sun. It lights Earth. Plants need light from the sun to grow. We use light from the sun to see.

4 **Mark (✔) what is not getting any sunlight.**

5 Read. As a class, talk about why it is important to be careful in the sun.

Out in the Sun

The sun can **harm** us, too. It is important to be careful in the sun. Too much sun can hurt your skin and eyes.

Sunscreen and a hat can protect you from the sun. Some **sunglasses** can protect your eyes from the sun. Never look directly at the sun.

6 Circle three things that protect these children from the sun.

Flash Lab

Heat from the Sun

Get two pieces of play dough. Put one piece in sunlight. Put the other in shade. Wait 10 minutes. Say how each feels.

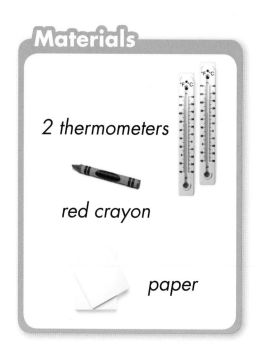

2 thermometers

red crayon

paper

Let's Investigate!

How can the sun make temperatures change?

1. Observe the thermometers.

2. Put one in sunlight. Put one in shade.

3. Wait and observe.

4. Draw two thermometers and mark the temperatures in red.

5. Think and tell how sunlight changed the temperature.

REVIEW THE BIG ?

What can you say about Earth and sky?

What is on Earth?

1 Circle the word that best completes each sentence

1. **Plains / Hills** are large, flat areas of land.
2. **Hills / Mountains** are where the land gets higher.
3. **Mountains / Islands** are the highest kind of land.

What changes land?

2 Underline the sentences that are true about volcanoes.

1. They cause slow land changes.
2. They can explode.
3. Their ash and rocks can cover land.

What is the sun?

3 Cross out (✘) the statement that tells how the sun harms us.

☐ It warms the land, water, and air.

☐ It can hurt our eyes and skin.

☐ It lights Earth.

Unit 6

Weather

 How can you describe weather?

1 Mark (✔) the picture that shows it is about to rain.

2 Look and circle the items you use on a rainy day.

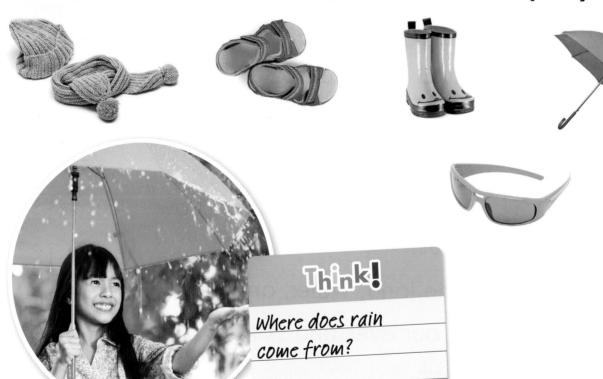

Think!

Where does rain come from?

Lesson 1 · What is weather?

1 **Read, look, and circle the words that describe the weather in the picture.**

Key Words

- weather
- storm
- safe
- thunderstorm
- shelter
- tornado
- hurricane
- snowstorm

Weather

Weather is what it is like outside. The weather changes from day to day. It may be windy or still. It may be wet or dry. It may be sunny or cloudy.

sunny   wet   cold   dry   cloudy   still

2 **Read, look, and match.**

Fluffy white clouds are a sign of good weather.

Dark clouds bring storms.

3 **Read, look at the pictures, and say the type of storm.**

Safety in Bad Weather

Storms can bring bad weather. You can stay **safe** during storms.

A **thunderstorm** has rain, lightning, and thunder. You can find **shelter** in a building or a car.

A **tornado** can happen during a thunderstorm. Tornadoes have very strong winds. They spin very fast. Go to a basement or a place without windows.

Flash Lab

Weather Safety
Put on a skit. Show the class how to stay safe in stormy weather.

4 **Circle T (true) or F (false).**

1. Storms bring good weather.   T / F
2. Find shelter in a building or car in a thunderstorm. T / F
3. Tornadoes have weak winds.   T / F
4. You can be safe in a basement in a tornado.   T / F

5 **Read and describe what the weather is like in a hurricane.**

A **hurricane** is a very bad storm. The wind blows very hard. The rain is very heavy. You can be safe in a hurricane. You should stay inside and away from windows.

6 **Read and draw one thing you need during a snowstorm.**

Snowstorms can bring lots of snow. Stay inside during a snowstorm. You can prepare for a snowstorm. You will need to have plenty of food and water.

Think!

When does a cloud make rain, and when does it make snow?

Lesson 2 · How can you measure weather?

1 **Read. Look at the picture and mark (✔) one thing the girl might do.**

Key Words

- measure
- tool
- thermometer
- temperature
- rain gauge
- wind vane

Measure Weather

People do different things in different kinds of weather. They may swim on a hot day. They may ice-skate on a cold day.

Some people **measure** the weather. They use weather **tools**. The tools help them know what the weather is like.

☐ swim   ☐ build a snowman   ☐ go fishing

2 **Look and circle the tool that measures rain.**

3 **Read. Look and circle the thermometer that matches the weather in the picture.**

Weather Tools

A **thermometer** is a weather tool. It measures temperature. **Temperature** is how hot or cold something is. The numbers on a thermometer show the temperature. The red line goes up as the air gets warmer. The red line goes down as the air gets cooler.

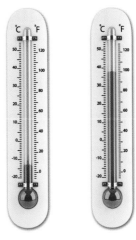

You can measure temperature in degrees Fahrenheit and degrees Celsius.

4 **Read and match the texts to the tools.**

More Weather Tools

A **rain gauge** measures rain. Rain falls into the top of the gauge. The numbers on it tell how much rain has fallen.

Wind moves the air. A **wind vane** points into the wind. It shows the direction the wind is coming from.

5 **Look. With a partner, say three words to describe the weather in the picture.**

Lesson 3 · What are the four seasons?

1 **Look and circle the picture that looks most like the season outside now.**

Key Words
- season

Spring

A **season** is a time of year. The four seasons are spring, summer, fall, and winter.

Spring comes after winter. It is warmer than winter. It might be rainy. Rain helps plants grow. Many animals have babies in spring.

2 **Read and write the season that comes after winter.**

Crocodiles lay their eggs in spring.

3 **Read and say the season in each picture.**

Summer and Fall

Summer comes after spring. It is warmer than spring. It can be very dry. Many plants and baby animals grow in the summer.

Fall comes after summer. It is cooler than summer. In the fall, some leaves change colors. Some animals store food for winter.

4 **Read and underline the correct word.**

a. Spring is **warmer / cooler** than summer.

b. Summer can be very **dry / wet.**

c. Fall comes **before / after** winter.

5 **What is fall like where you live? Say as a class.**

I Will Know...

6 **Read. With a partner, describe winter where you live.**

Winter

Winter comes after fall. It can be the coldest season. It snows in some places.

Some plants die in winter. Some animals grow thick fur. The fur keeps them warm.

Thick fur keeps the rabbit warm in winter.

7 **Draw what winter is like where you live.**

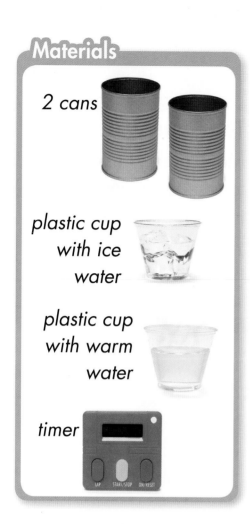

Materials

2 cans

plastic cup with ice water

plastic cup with warm water

timer

Let's Investigate!

How does water vapor condense?

1. Fill one can halfway with ice water. Fill the other can halfway with warm water.

2. Observe the outside of each can. Record what you observe.

3. Wait 5 minutes.

4. Record the changes you see on the outside of each can.

Outside of Can		
	At Beginning	**After 5 Minutes**
Warm water		
Ice water		

Lesson 1

What is weather?

1 Circle how you stay safe in a hurricane.

a) Go outside.

b) Stay inside, away from the windows.

c) Stay inside a car.

Lesson 2

How can you measure weather?

2 Circle the tool you can use to measure temperature.

Lesson 3

What are the four seasons?

3 Circle the words that describe summer in the picture.

wet   cold   dry   still

sunny   windy   warm   rainy   cloudy

How can you describe matter?

I will learn

- about matter and mass.
- to describe objects by their properties.
- to identify solids, liquids, and gases.
- ways matter can change.

1 **Cross out (✗) one thing you do not need to make bubbles.**

liquid soap

bubble wand

sponge

plastic jar

water

2 **With a partner, say how to make bubbles.**

Think!

What is inside the bubble?

Lesson 1 · What is matter?

1 **Read and underline the sentence that tells what mass is.**

Matter

Matter is anything that takes up space. It has mass. **Mass** is the amount of matter in an object. The table is matter and has mass.

2 **Look. What objects have more mass than the blocks? Say as a class.**

3 **Complete the sentences with words from the text.**

a) Matter takes up _____.

b) The table has _____.

4 **Read. Look at the picture and match the columns.**

Objects and Matter

All objects are made of matter. You can describe objects in many ways. Objects can be different colors, sizes, and shapes. They can be hard or soft. The red marble is round and hard.

a) It is round and purple.

b) It is long, soft, and blue.

c) It is big, soft, and brown.

scarf

teddy bear

ball

5 **Choose one object from the scene and describe it to a partner.**

6 **Read. With a partner, talk about one way you can group objects.**

Describe and Group Objects

Objects can feel different. The wall feels smooth. Objects can be heavy or light. **Weight** is how heavy an object is. A pile of books can be heavy. You can group objects by how they are alike. Marbles can be small and round. They are alike.

7 **Look at the balls. Circle the one that has the greatest mass.**

8 **Write 1, 2, and 3 to order the balls from heavy to light.**

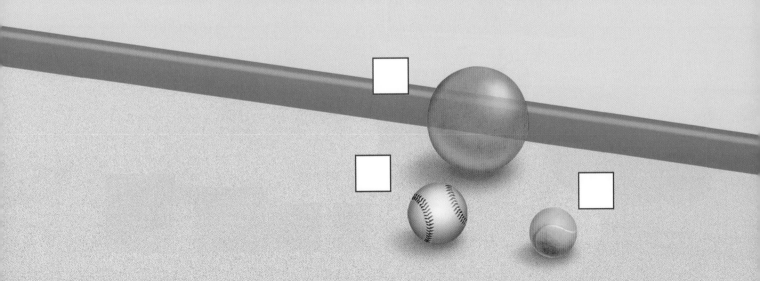

9 **Read. Underline the meanings of _float_ and _sink_.**

More Ways to Describe Objects

Objects can float or sink. **Float** means to stay on top of a liquid. **Sink** means to fall to the bottom of a liquid. Lemonade is a liquid. The ice cubes float in the lemonade. Objects can be different temperatures. The lemonade is cold. People use different materials to make objects. The oven is metal. The timer is plastic.

10 **Look at the picture and circle something that sinks.**

11 **Mark (✔) something people made out of plastic.**

12 **Cross out (✗) something that is hot.**

Think!

Why do the ice cubes float in the lemonade?

Lesson 2 · What are solids, liquids, and gases?

Key Words
- solid
- liquid
- gas
- freeze
- melt
- boil

1 **Read. With a partner, say two details about solids.**

Solids

Matter can be a solid, liquid, or gas. A **solid** has its own shape and size. A solid does not change shape when you move it. The box is a solid. The toys are solids.

2 **Does the shape of the teddy bear change if you pick it up? Discuss as a class.**

3 **Think of a solid object in your bedroom. Draw it.**

4 Read. With a partner, tell one way liquids and gases are alike.

Liquids and Gases

A **liquid** takes the shape of its container. You can pour a liquid. Water is a liquid. A gas can change shape and size. It takes the shape of its container. A **gas** fills all of its container. You cannot see most gases. Air is a gas.

5 Look and circle something that contains a liquid.

6 What happens to the lemonade inside the containers? Discuss as a class.

7 Mark (✔) the objects filled with gas.

8 **Read. With a partner, say why water freezes and ice melts.**

How Matter Changes

Matter can change form. Water freezes into ice when it gets very cold. **Freeze** means to change from a liquid to a solid. Ice melts when it gets warm. **Melt** means to change from a solid to a liquid. Water can evaporate when it boils. **Boil** means to heat a liquid until it becomes a gas.

9 **Look at the liquid that is changing into a gas. Mark (✔) why this happens.**

☐ The liquid is melting.

☐ The liquid is freezing.

☐ The liquid is boiling.

10 **Look at the picture. Circle a solid that can melt in the sun.**

Lesson 3 · How can matter change?

Key Words
- ash
- iron
- rust
- oxygen

1 **Read and circle how matter can change.**

Changes in Matter

Matter can change. The color, size, and shape of matter can change.

2 **Look. With a partner, talk about how the popcorn changes.**

3 **Read. Why can you bend a straw? Say with a partner.**

Bend and Cut

You can bend a plastic straw. It changes shape. It is still plastic. You can cut and fold paper. It changes shape. It does not change color. It is still paper.

4 **What stays the same when you cut paper? Discuss as a class.**

5 **Read. How can wood change to a different kind of matter? Say with a partner.**

Different Matter

Matter changes into different kinds of matter. Wood can burn. It changes color. It changes to **ash**, water, and gas. It will not change back into wood. **Iron** can turn into rust. It might turn into rust when it gets wet. **Rust** is a kind of matter. Iron and oxygen make up rust. **Oxygen** is a gas in the air. Iron is strong. Rust breaks easily. Rust will not change back into iron.

At-Home Lab

Objects Change

Look around your home. Find ways people change matter. Say how they change it.

6 **Look and match.**

ash   rust

Materials

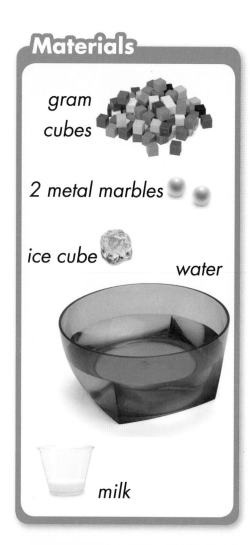

gram cubes

2 metal marbles

ice cube

water

milk

Let's Investigate!

How are objects different?

1. Observe all the objects.

2. Classify the objects.
Put the solid objects together.
Put the liquid objects together.

3. Classify each object as hard or wet. Use the chart. Make an **✗** for each object.

Observations		
	Hard	**Wet**
Gram cubes		
Metal marbles		
Ice cube		
Water		
Milk		

Lesson 1

What is matter?

1 Draw one thing that has more mass than a pencil.

Lesson 2

What are solids, liquids, and gases?

2 Circle the correct word.

a) Freezing changes a **liquid / gas** into a solid.

b) **Boiling / Melting** changes a liquid into a gas.

Lesson 3

How can matter change?

3 Circle the word that does not belong.

a) When wood burns, it changes to

ash, water, rust, and gas.

b) Rust is a kind of matter made from

iron, ash, and oxygen.

Unit 8 Energy

 **What can energy do?**

I will learn

- how to use energy.
- what light can do.
- how to make sounds.

1 Circle what gives energy.

2 Mark (✔) the objects that use energy.

3 Look at the picture. Complete the sentence.

big   hot   cold

The coals in the grill

are ✎ _____ .

Think!

What makes food cook on a grill?

Lesson 1 · How do we use energy?

Key Words
- electricity
- energy
- fuel
- gasoline
- engine
- battery
- key

1 **Read and look at the picture. Tell what things use energy.**

Energy

Click! You turn on the lamp. Electricity makes the lamp glow. The lamp will not glow without electricity. **Electricity** is a kind of energy. **Energy** can cause change or do work.

2 **Complete the chart.**

Cause		Effect
The lamp has no electricity.	→	It _____ _____ _____ .

3 Read. What gives a car the energy to move? Say with a partner.

Cars and Energy

Cars use energy. Most cars get energy from **fuel**. The fuel burns to make heat or power. Cars use **gasoline** for fuel. A car's **engine** burns the gasoline. The car has energy to move.

4 Look at the picture and complete the sentence.

gasoline   cars

_____ get _____ from gas pumps.

5 Circle the part of the car that burns the gasoline.

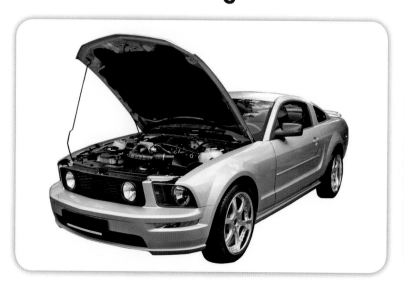

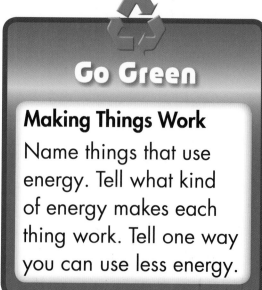

Go Green

Making Things Work
Name things that use energy. Tell what kind of energy makes each thing work. Tell one way you can use less energy.

6 **Read. Where does the waterwheel get energy from? Say with a partner.**

Using Energy

Moving water has energy. It turns the waterwheel in the picture. **Batteries** store energy. Batteries change the stored energy into electricity. The toy car uses electricity to move. Wind the **key**. The robot stores energy as you wind. Let go of the key. The robot moves. The stored energy changes to moving energy.

7 **What do batteries do with their stored energy? Discuss as a class.**

8 **Write where each toy gets energy from.**

_____   _____

_____   _____

Lesson 2. What is light?

Key Words
- light
- shadow

1 **Read. Draw one more object that makes light.**

What Makes Light

Light is a kind of energy. We can see light energy. Light comes from the sun, other stars, candles, and lamps, too.

2 **Match the texts with the pictures.**

Fireflies make their own light.

Fireworks explode and give off light.

3 Read. Why can you see light in the lantern? Say with a partner.

Light Shines Through

Light passes through a window and thin paper. It will not pass through you. You make a shadow. A **shadow** forms when something blocks the light.

4 Circle the objects light can pass through.

5 What causes a shadow? Discuss as a class.

6 Draw yourself and your shadow.

7 **Read. Why can you see yourself in a mirror? Say with a partner.**

What Can Light Do

Light travels in a straight line. It bounces off objects that are smooth and shiny. Light bounces back to you from a mirror. That is why you can see yourself.

8 **Look at the pictures. How do the shapes of the objects change what you see? Discuss as a class.**

9 **Mark (✔) the objects light bounces off.**

Lesson 3 · What is sound?

1 **Read. With a partner, think of objects that vibrate and make sound.**

Sounds

Sound is a kind of energy. We can hear sound energy. Sound comes from objects that vibrate. **Vibrate** means to move back and forth very fast. The girl plucks the guitar strings. You hear sounds when the strings vibrate.

2 **Look at the picture. Write what happens when the girl plucks the guitar strings.**

vibrate   sound   strings

The ✎ _____ ✎ _____

_____

and make ✎ _____.

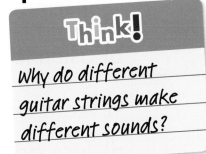

3 **What do the players need to do to make their instruments make sound? Say with a partner.**

Think!

why do different guitar strings make different sounds?

4 Read and circle the sentence that tells how sounds can be.

Loud and Soft

Listen to the sounds around you. Some sounds are **loud**, and some are **soft**. The ringing of a school bell is loud. The chirp of a baby bird is soft.

5 Write *S* (soft) or *L* (loud) depending on whether the object makes a soft or a loud sound.

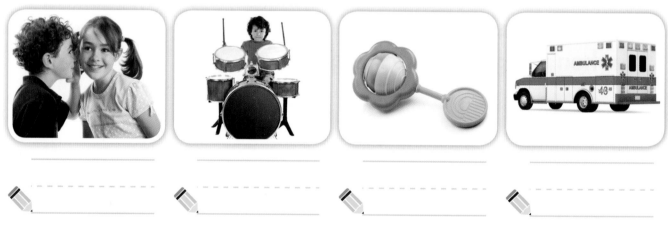

6 Mark (✔) the sentences that tell how to protect your ears from loud sounds.

a) Wear earmuffs in places where noisy equipment is used.

b) Listen to your music player at a very loud volume.

c) Use earplugs when you're listening to live music.

d) Turn down the volume on your TV.

7 Read. Circle the photo of something that makes a low sound.

High and Low

Some sounds are **high**. Others are **low**. You can sing a song in a high voice. You can sing a song in a low voice.

8 As a class, think of things that make low or high sounds.

2 bottles
with water

B C

A

1 almost empty bottle

Let's Investigate!

What sounds can bottles make?

1. Blow over the top of Bottle A. Listen to the sound.

2. Repeat Step 1 with Bottle B and Bottle C.

3. Record the sounds you hear.

Sounds from Each Bottle	
Bottle	**Sound**
A (almost empty)	
B (half full)	
C (almost full)	

Unit 8
Review

REVIEW THE BIG ? **What can energy do?**

How do we use energy?

1 Underline the sentence about energy that is not true.

a) People burn fuel to make a car move.

b) Toys without plugs can use batteries for electricity.

c) Bicycles need electricity.

What is light?

2 Circle the words that complete the sentence.

Light bounces off things that are _____ and _____.

| dark   shiny   rough   smooth   flat |

What is sound?

3 Complete the sentences to show what happens when things vibrate.

Cause ⟶ **Effect**

Things ✎ _____. They make ✎ _____.

> Got it? Quiz   > Got it? Self Assessment   Unit 8   **99**

Unit 9 Movement

How can you describe ways objects move?

I will learn

- how objects can move.
- how forces change the way things move.
- that gravity pulls objects toward Earth.

1 Circle what is moving each object.

2 Mark (✔) the objects you can move easily.

 books

 ball

 blocks

 bricks

Think!

what happens when a dog sticks its head out of a window?

Lesson 1 · How can objects move?

Key Words
- move
- straight
- curved
- around
- zigzag
- speed
- quickly
- slowly

1 **Read. What are three ways objects can move? Say with a partner.**

Ways to Move

Objects can **move** in many ways. They can move in a **straight** line. A car can move in a straight line. Objects can move in a **curved** line. A roller coaster moves in a curved line. Objects can move **around** and around in a circle. A merry-go-round moves around and around.

2 **Match the columns to show how the objects move.**

Around and around.

In a straight line.

In a curved line.

3 **Read. With a partner, say other ways things can move.**

More Ways to Move

Objects can start to move. They can roll and slide. Objects can move back and forth. Some move in a **zigzag**.

4 **Match the texts with the pictures.**

People walk in a zigzag down this path.

The children spin around and around in circles.

5 **What is speed? Say with a partner.**

Speed

Speed is how **quickly** or **slowly** an object moves. Some objects move fast. Others move slowly. Objects can stop.

6 **Mark (✔) the objects that move slowly and cross out (✘) the ones that move fast.**

Lesson 2 · What is a force?

Key Words
- force
- push
- pull
- direction
- motion

1 **Read. Mark (✔) the box to show if the picture shows a push or a pull.**

Force

A **force** is a **push** or a **pull**. You use forces every day. You pull a drawer open. You push a drawer closed.

Object	Push	Pull

2 **Draw something you push.**

3 **Draw something you pull.**

4 **Read. What can a force do? Say as a class.**

What a Force Can Do

A force can change how objects move.
It can start an object moving. A force can
stop a moving object. A force can change
the **direction** of a moving object.

5 **Read the sentences and number the pictures.**

1. A force can change the direction of an object.

2. A force can stop a moving object.

3. A force can start an object moving.

Think!

How can the children stop the ball from moving?

6 **Read. What is motion? Say with a partner.**

More Force, Less Force

Motion is the act of moving. Use more force. The motion of an object changes more. Use less force. The motion of an object changes less.

7 **Look at the pictures. How can the mother change the motion of the swing less? How can the boy change the motion of the bike more? Say as a class.**

8 **Draw yourself stopping a moving object.**

Lesson 2 Check   ▷   Got it?   60-Second Video

Lesson 3 · What is gravity?

1 **Read. What is gravity? Say with a partner.**

Key Words
- gravity
- ground

Pull of Gravity

Earth pulls objects down. This pull is called **gravity**. Gravity is a force. It pulls objects on or near Earth toward it. Gravity keeps you on the **ground**. It keeps your desk on the floor.

2 **Look at the picture. Write what will happen to the ball.**

toward   ground   drop

The ball will

the

3 **Read. Why does the kite stay up? Say with a partner.**

Hold Up

Gravity pulls objects toward Earth unless something holds them up. Gravity pulls on the kite. The wind holds up the kite. Gravity pulls on the roll of string. The boy holds up the roll of string.

4 **Draw yourself holding up a balloon. Why does it stay up? Say as a class.**

5 **Read. How does the water move as it comes out of the fountain? Say with a partner.**

Pull Down

Gravity can pull objects without touching them. The water shoots out of the fountain. Nothing holds the water up. Gravity pulls the water down without touching it.

6 **Draw an arrow to show what happens to the kite when the wind stops holding it up.**

At-Home Lab

Gravity and Air

Get two sheets of paper. Make one sheet into a ball. Hold it in one hand. Hold the second sheet in your other hand. Drop them at the same time. Tell what happens.

Materials

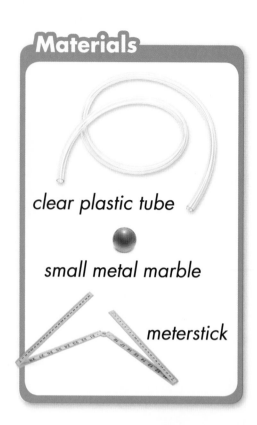

clear plastic tube

small metal marble

meterstick

Let's Investigate!

How do objects move?

1. Drop a marble in a curved tube.

2. Measure how far the marble rolls out. Record.

3. Make the tube straight. Drop the marble in the tube.

4. Measure and record.

Distance Rolled	
Shape of Tube	**How far did the marble roll? (cm)**
Curved	
Straight	

Lesson 1

How can objects move?

1 Draw lines to show each way of moving.

| zigzag | straight | in a circle | curved |

Lesson 2

What is a force?

2 Circle *T* (true) or *F* (false).

1. You need to move your legs more to run faster. **T/F**
2. You need less force to push a cart than a toy car. **T/F**
3. You need more force to pull a pony than a toy wagon. **T/F**
4. You don't need force to stop a swing. **T/F**

Lesson 3

What is gravity?

3 Draw what will happen next.

Unit 1   The Design Process

cotton The material made from the white hair of the cotton plant.

discovery A fact or thing that someone finds out about that was not known before.

goal Something you want to do.

label A word used to describe something, for example, in a picture.

material What something is made of. Wood is a good material for a house.

natural Something that is in nature and is not made by people.

plan The way you will solve a problem.

plastic A material made by people that can be hard or soft.

problem A question you want to find an answer to.

rock Rock is the hard material that forms the surface of the Earth.

science Knowledge about the world, especially from looking and testing.

scientists People who use technology to make discoveries about the world.

solution An answer to a problem.

technology The use of science to help solve problems.

wood The material trees are made of.

Unit 2   Living Things and Their Environments

air The mixture of gases around Earth, which plants and animals need to live.

desert A land environment that is very dry.

environment All the living and nonliving things in one place.

forest A land environment that has many trees.

light The energy from the sun. Plants need light to make food.

marsh A wetland that has grasses.

need Something a living thing has to have to live.

nutrient Any material living things need to live and grow.

ocean A large body of salty water.

prairie A land environment that is flat and covered with grasses.

shelter A safe place to live and grow. Beavers build their own shelter.

soil The dirt in which plants grow. Plants get nutrients from the soil.

swamp A wetland environment that has soft, wet land and can have many trees.

water The clear liquid without color, smell, or taste that falls as rain. Water is used for drinking.

wetland A land environment that is partly covered with water or is wet most of the time.

Glossary   **113**

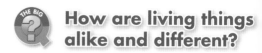

Unit 3   Plants and Animals

alike   The same in some way.

amphibian   An animal that has a backbone and smooth, wet skin.

backbone   The set of bones along the middle of the back of some animals.

cone   Some plants, like pine trees, have cones that make seeds.

different   Not the same in some way.

fuzzy   Covered with soft, short hairs.

herd   A group of animals of one kind that stays together.

insect   An animal that does not have a backbone and has six legs.

mammal   An animal that has a backbone. Most mammals have fur or hair.

parent   A living thing that has young, like the father or mother of a person or animal.

petunia   A kind of plant that has fuzzy, green leaves and pink, purple, or white flowers.

reptile   An animal that has a backbone and dry skin and scales.

seed   What plants make so new plants of the same kind can grow. Plants with flowers make seeds.

shape   The form that something has, for example, round or square. Animals often have the same shape as their parents.

young   A living thing that is in the early part of its life. A dog's young is called a puppy.

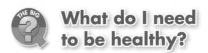
Unit 4 Body and Health

bandage A piece of cloth you put on a cut to keep it clean.

cavity A hole in something. We can get cavities in our teeth.

cut A hole or wound made by a sharp object.

checkup Something a doctor or dentist gives you regularly to make sure you are healthy.

eating well Eating food that keeps you healthy.

exercise Physical activities that you do to stay healthy and become stronger.

germ A very small thing that can grow inside your body and cause disease, or make you sick.

habit Something we do over and over again.

heal To become healthy again.

healthy Strong and not sick or injured. When your body is working well, you are healthy.

life jacket A piece of clothing worn around your upper body to stop you from sinking in the water.

nutrient Material in food that your body uses to repair itself and to grow.

skin The layer that covers your body.

sneeze (v) To let air out of your nose in a very sudden and noisy way.

sunscreen A cream, lotion, or spray that can keep your skin safe, or protect it, from the sun.

Unit 5   Earth and Sky

earthquake A sudden shaking of Earth's surface that often causes a lot of damage.

erosion What happens when wind or water moves rocks and soil.

gas The material stars, like the sun, are made of.

harm (v) To hurt.

heat The warmth the sun gives to living and nonliving things on Earth.

hill An area of land that is higher than the land around it. A hill is like a mountain but smaller.

island A piece of land with water all around it.

lake A large area of water that has land all around it.

mountain A very high hill. A mountain is the highest kind of land.

plain A large, flat area of land.

river Water that flows in a long line across land.

star A celestial body made of hot gases.

sunglasses Dark glasses that can keep your eyes safe, or protect them, from the sun.

warm (v) To make the temperature of something a little hotter. The sun warms the land, the water, and the air.

weathering What happens when water or ice breaks rocks into smaller pieces.

wood The material trees are made of.

Unit 6   Weather

hurricane A very bad storm with strong winds and heavy rain.

measure (v) To find the size, length, or amount of something.

rain gauge A tool that measures how much rain falls.

safe To keep away from any physical injury or harm. You can stay safe from bad weather.

season One of the four periods during a year. Each season has its own type of weather. Winter, spring, summer, and fall are seasons.

shelter A place you can stay dry and safe in bad weather.

snowstorm A storm that brings lots of snow and can have strong winds.

storm A period of bad weather when there is a lot of rain, snow, strong winds, or lightning.

temperature The measure of how hot or cold something is. A thermometer tells you the temperature.

thermometer A tool that measures temperature.

thunderstorm A storm with rain, thunder, and lightning.

tool A thing that helps you do something, like measure the weather.

tornado A bad storm in which strong winds spin very fast.

weather How hot or cold, wet or dry, and windy or still it is outside.

wind vane A tool that shows what direction the wind is coming from.

Unit 7   Matter

ash   The solid matter left after something is burned.

boil (v)   To heat a liquid until it becomes gas.

float (v)   To stay on top of a liquid without sinking.

freeze (v)   To change from a liquid to a solid.

gas   A material, like air, that fills all of its container. It usually cannot be seen.

iron   A common metal that is strong but can rust.

liquid   A material that is not a solid or a gas and that takes the shape of its container.

mass   The amount of matter in an object.

matter   The material that everything is made of. Matter takes up space.

melt (v)   To change from a solid to a liquid.

oxygen   A gas in the air. It combines with iron to make rust.

rust   The reddish brown material that is made of iron and oxygen.

sink (v)   To fall below the top or to the bottom of a liquid.

solid   A firm object or material that does not change its shape.

weight   How heavy an object is.